Collins

Treasure House

Pupil Book 5

Spelling Skills

Authors: Sarah Snashall and Chris Whitney

William Collins' dream of knowledge for all began with the publication of his first book in 1819.

A self-educated mill worker, he not only enriched millions of lives, but also founded a flourishing publishing house. Today, staying true to this spirit, Collins books are packed with inspiration, innovation and practical expertise. They place you at the centre of a world of possibility and give you exactly what you need to explore it.

Collins. Freedom to teach.

Published by Collins
An imprint of HarperCollinsPublishers
The News Building
1 London Bridge Street
London
SE1 9GF

Browse the complete Collins catalogue at
www.collins.co.uk

British Library Cataloguing in Publication Data

A Catalogue record for this publication is available from the British Library

Publishing Director: Lee Newman
Publishing Manager: Helen Doran
Senior Editor: Hannah Dove
Project Manager: Emily Hooton
Authors: Sarah Snashall and Chris Whitney
Development Editor: Jessica Marshall
Copy-editor: Ros & Chris Davies
Proofreader: Tracy Thomas
Cover design and artwork: Amparo Barrera and Ken Vail Graphic Design
Internal design concept: Amparo Barrera
Typesetter: Jouve India Private Ltd
Illustrations: Caroline Romanet, Aptara and QBS
Production Controller: Rachel Weaver

Printed and bound by Grafica Veneta S.p.A., Italy

Acknowledgements

The publishers wish to thank the following for permission to reproduce photographs. Every effort has been made to trace copyright holders and to obtain their permission for the use of copyright materials. The publishers will gladly receive any information enabling them to rectify any error or omission at the first opportunity.

p11 GraphicsRF/Shutterstock, p13 studiolaut/Shutterstock, p19 Bert Gravy/Shutterstock, p21 Andrii Bezvershenko/Shutterstock, p26 300 librarians/Shutterstock, p27 Merfin/Shutterstock, p33t Spreadthesig/Shutterstock, p33b Chubarov Alexandr/Shutterstock, p32 GraphicsRF/Shutterstock, p34 Lorelyn Medina/Shutterstock, p35 Visual Generation/Shutterstock, p37 Iconic Bestiary/Shutterstock, p48 Neizu/Shutterstock, p49 mistery/Shutterstock.

Contents

The suffixes −cious and −tious

When adding the ending **−ious** to a word, it is sometimes difficult to remember whether to spell it **−cious** or **−tious** because both spell **/shus/**.

If the root word ends **−ce**, the ending is **−cious**. Remove the **e** before adding **−ious**: grac**e** + **ious** = grac**ious**.

If the root word ends **−tion**, the ending is **−tious**. Remove the **−ion** before adding **−ious**: caut**ion** + **ious** = caut**ious**.

There is one common exception: anx**ious** (meaning: nervous).

Get started

Copy and complete the table, sorting these words into words ending **−cious** and words ending **−tious**. One has been done for you.

1. scrumptious
2. cautious
3. precious
4. conscious
5. delicious
6. ambitious
7. fictitious
8. unambitious
9. incautious
10. ferocious

Words ending **−cious**	Words ending **−tious**
	scrumptious

Try these

Add the suffix **–cious** or **–tious** to these words. Consider the ending of the root word before you add the suffix. One has been done for you.

1. vice

    Answer: *vicious*

2. ambition

3. malice

4. space

5. infection

6. nutrition

7. superstition

8. pretention

9. grace

10. contention

Now try these

Use the words below in sentences of your own. An example has been done for you.

ferocious, fictitious, anxious, cautious, unambitious, scrumptious, precious, unconscious, delicious, incautious

> Answer: *Beneath the waves lurks a ferocious monster.*

The suffixes –cial and –tial

Some words end with the suffixes **–cial** and **–tial**. After a vowel, use the ending **–cial**. After a consonant, use the ending **–tial**.

There are some exceptions. For example, finan**cial**, commer**cial**, provin**cial**. For these, it can help to remember the root nouns: finan**ce**, commer**ce** and provin**ce**.

There are many **–cial** exceptions, however, that just have to be learned. For example, benefi**cial**

The exception **initial** has no root word, so it just needs to be learned.

Get started

Copy the table. Sort these words into two groups: words ending **–cial** and words ending **–tial**. One has been done for you.

1. torrential

2. financial

3. partial

4. special

5. artificial

6. provincial

7. social

8. initial

9. commercial

10. unofficial

Words ending **–cial**	Words ending **–tial**
	torrential

Try these

Choose the correct suffix to complete each of these words. One has been done for you.

1. fa (–cial / –tial)

   Answer: *facial*

2. residen (–cial / –tial)

3. circumstan (–cial / –tial)

4. gla (–cial / –tial)

5. insubstan (–cial / –tial)

6. superfi (–cial / –tial)

7. poten (–cial / –tial)

8. cru (–cial / –tial)

9. ra (–cial / –tial)

10. mar (–cial / –tial)

Now try these

Copy and complete the sentences by choosing the correct spelling of each missing word. One has been done for you.

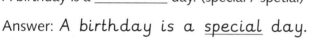

1. A birthday is a _____ day. (special / spetial)

   Answer: A birthday is a special day.

2. This information is _____. (confidencial / confidential)

3. Water is _____ to life. (essencial / essential)

4. A smile is a type of _____ expression. (facial / fatial)

5. The evidence against the defendant is _____. (circumstancial / circumstantial)

6. The ogre's aggressive behaviour was _____. (antisocial / antisotial)

7. Many communities are _____. (multiracial / multiratial)

8. Exercise is _____ to one's health. (beneficial / benefitial)

9. Sanjeev was the _____ winner of the tournament. (official / offitial)

10. The company faced _____ ruin. (financial / finantial)

The suffixes –ant and –ent

The endings **–ant** and **–ent** sound similar. Use **–ant** if there is a related word with an **/ay/** sound in the right position. The ending **–ation** is often a clue. For example, hesit**ation**, hesit**ant**

Use **–ent** after the soft **/s/** sound, after the soft **/j/** sound, or if there is a related word with a clear **/e/** sound in the right position. For example, inno**cent**, a**gent**, confid**ential** – confid**ent**

There are many words, however, that just have to be learned. Examples include assist**ant**, obedi**ent** and independ**ent**.

Get started

Copy the table. Sort these words into two groups: words ending **–ant** and words ending **–ent**.

1. attendant
2. independent
3. innocent
4. confident
5. agent
6. hesitant
7. obedient
8. observant
9. decent
10. servant

Words ending **–ant**	Words ending **–ent**
attendant	

Try these

Choose the correct spellings of the words below. One has been done for you.

1. important / importent

   Answer: *important*

2. tolerant / tolerent

3. expectant / expectent

4. magnificant / magnificent

5. absant / absent

6. differant / different

7. urgant / urgent

8. intelligant / intelligent

9. radiant / radient

10. president / presidant

Now try these

Use each word from the 'Try these' activity in a sentence of your own. An example has been done for you.

Answer: *The children studied for an important exam.*

The suffixes −ence, −ency, −ance and −ancy

The endings **−ance** and **−ence** sound similar, as do the endings **−ency** and **−ancy**. If there is a related word with an **−ant** or **−ent** ending, the **a** or **e** spelling will be consistent.

import**ant** → import**ance**

urg**ent** → urg**ency**

Words ending **−ence**, **−ency**, **−ance** or **−ancy** are nouns. Most words will take only one ending or the other, though some have both:

hesitant	hesitance	hesitancy
~~appearant~~	appearance	~~appearancy~~
urgent	~~urgence~~	urgency

Get started

Write these words as pairs, matching the adjectives to their related nouns. Underline the ending of each word. One has been done for you.

1. innocent		confidence
2. urgent		silence
3. elegant		urgency
4. confident		elegance
5. different		vacancy
6. brilliant		difference
7. silent		brilliance
8. vacant		innocence

Answer: *innoc<u>ent</u>   innoc<u>ence</u>*

Try these

Copy and complete the sentences by choosing the correct spelling for each missing word. One has been done for you.

1. Mia and Tia were wearing the same jumper – what a _____! (coincidents / coincidence)

   Answer: Mia and Tia were wearing the same jumper – what a <u>coincidence</u>!

2. Put all the _____ in a bowl and mix them together. (ingredients / ingredience)

3. I know you ate the cake because the _____ is all around your mouth! (evidents / evidence)

4. The _____ destroyed the undergrowth. (elephants / elephance)

5. The _____ clapped loudly at the end of the show. (audients / audience)

6. The _____ lined up to meet the new master of the manor. (servants / servance)

Now try these

Read the pairs of words and decide which words exist. Write the correct words. One has been done for you.

1. frequence   frequency

   Answer: *frequency*

2. audience   audiency

3. performance   performancy

4. decence   decency

5. resistance   resistancy

6. Presidence   Presidency

7. defence   defency

8. pregnance   pregnancy

Common words (1)

In English there are many words with double letters. You have to learn which letters to double.

Get started

Copy and complete the table, sorting these words into three groups: words with a double **m**, words with a double **c** and words with a double **p**. One has been done for you.

committee

appreciate

community

accompany

accommodate

apparent

communicate

immediate

according

Double **m**	Double **c**	Double **p**
committee		

Try these

These words should all have a double letter. Can you remember which letter? Choose the correct spelling of each word. One has been done for you.

1. attached   atacched

    Answer: *attached*

2. exccelent   excellent

3. exaggerate   exagerrate

4. embarass   embarrass

5. correspond   coresppond

6. acomppany   accompany

7. aggressive   agressive

8. immediate   imeddiate

Now try these

Copy and complete the sentences, filling in the missing letter or letters. One has been done for you.

1. I'm so emba____a____ed!

    Answer: *I'm so embarrassed!*

2. Come here i____e____iately!

3. Can you a____om____any us, please?

4. That is e____e____ent!

5. Ravi and Ben are on the co____i____ee.

6. A____or____ing to Casey, you have my ball.

The suffixes –able, –ible, –ably and –ibly

Some adjectives end with the letters **–able** or **–ible**. Their related adverbs end with the letters **–ably** or **–ibly**. The **–able** / **–ably** endings are far more common than the **–ible** / **–ibly** endings and are usually used if a complete root word can be heard before it. For example, **depend**able, **depend**ably; **reli**able, **reli**ably

The **–ible** / **–ibly** ending is common if a complete root word cannot be heard. For example, **horr**ible, **horr**ibly; **incred**ible, **incred**ibly

The word '**sens**ible' is an exception.

Get started

Copy and complete the table by filling in the missing root, related adjective and/or related adverb for each word. One has been done for you.

Root	Adjective	Adverb
comfort	comfortable	comfortably
consider		
	understandable	
		reasonably
	enjoyable	
laugh		

Try these

Choose the correct spelling of each word. One has been done for you.

1. possable / possible

   Answer: *possible*

2. incredable / incredible

3. reasonable / reasonible

4. honourable / honourible

5. terrable / terrible

6. edable / edible

7. horrable / horrible

8. visible / visable

9. dependable / dependible

10. bearable / bearible

Now try these

Change these verbs into adjectives or adverbs (your choice) and then use them in sentences of your own. An example has been done for you.

sense, consider, comfort, laugh, honour, bear, depend, avoid, afford

Answer: *"Line up sensibly," the teacher said.*

Adding suffixes beginning with vowels to words ending in –fer

When you add a suffix that starts with a vowel (for example, **–ed** or **–ing**) to a word ending in **–fer** (for example, pre**fer**), the spelling rule depends on which syllable is stressed.

If the second syllable is stressed (for example, pre**fer**), double the **r** when adding the suffix (prefe**rr**ed). If the second syllable is not stressed (for example, **of**fer), do not double the **r** (offered).

Get started

Add **–ed** to these words. Decide whether each word should be spelt with a single or a double **r**. One has been done for you.

1. suffer

   Answer: suffered

2. offer

3. prefer

4. refer

5. infer

Say the words aloud and decide whether or not the **–fer** syllable is stressed after adding the suffix. Sort the words into two groups: words where **–fer** is stressed and words where it is not.

–fer is stressed with suffix	–fer is not stressed with suffix

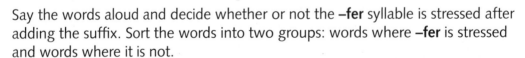

Try these

Choose the correct spelling of each word. One has been done for you.

1. suffering / sufferring

   Answer: *suffering*

2. offering / offerring

3. confering / conferring

4. prefering / preferring

5. reference / referrence

6. preference / preferrence

7. refering / referring

8. transfering / transferring

9. referal / referral

10. referee / referree

Now try these

Copy out this paragraph, deciding on the correct spellings to fill the gaps. One has been done for you.

The waiter *offered* the customers a drink. After **con_____ing** briefly, they said they normally **pre_____ed** to see the menu first. The waiter **re_____ed** them to the specials board, took their orders and, in **re_____ence** to the soup, made a note of the woman's **pre_____ence**. However, while **trans_____ing** their meal from tray to table, the waiter **suf_____ed** a fall. From the looks on their faces, the waiter **in_____ed** they would not give the restaurant a good **re_____al**.

Review unit 1

Can you remember the spellings you've learned this term? Answer these questions to find out.

A. Choose the correct spelling of each word.

1. spatious   spacious
2. artificial   artifitial
3. important   importent
4. accidant   accident
5. suitible   suitable
6. reference   referrence
7. reasonibly   reasonably
8. committee   committey

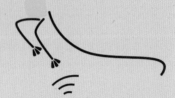

B. These words are all spelt incorrectly. Correct the spelling of each word.

1. accomoddate
2. corresspond
3. entrence
4. horrable
5. refered
6. delitious
7. urgancy
8. coresspond

C. Copy these sentences. Add one of the endings **–tial**, **–ed**, **–able**, **–ence**, **–ant** or **–ible** to complete the word in brackets in each sentence. Use each ending only once.

1. Sleeping on the floor is not very (comfort).

2. Listen, everyone, I have some (import) news.

3. Sacha (offer) her seat on the bus to the old man.

4. The comprehension exercise tested our use of (infer).

5. Megan is very (flex) and can easily touch her toes.

6. The (torrent) rain ruined our day out.

Common words (2)

Here are some more words with those tricky double letters to spell.

Get started

Write out these words and underline the double letter in each word. One has been done for you.

1. immediately

   Answer: _imm_ediately

2. interrupt

3. necessary

4. occupy

5. occur

6. opportunity

7. profession

8. programme

9. recommend

10. suggest

11. marvellous

Try these

Cover up the words in the 'Get started' activity. Copy and complete these words. One has been done for you.

1. o__ortu__ity

   Answer: *opportunity*

2. pro__ra__e

3. in__e__upt

4. marve__ous

5. o__upy

6. re__o__end

7. i__edia__ely

8. o__ur

9. ne__e__ary

10. pro__e__ion

11. su__est

Now try these

Copy and complete the sentences, choosing the correct spelling of the missing words. One has been done for you.

1. We had a _____ day out at the zoo.
   (marvelouss / marvellous)

   Answer: *We had a marvellous day out at the zoo.*

2. Please don't _____ me – I'm talking to Mrs Bishop.   (intterupt / interrupt)

3. It's cold and wet so I _____ you take a coat.
   (recommend / reccomend)

4. Ben slipped and, suddenly, Oliver had an _____ to score.   (opportunity / opportunitee)

5. It's going to be _____ to drive into town because we're late.
   (neccessary / necessary)

Use of the hyphen after prefixes

Hyphens can be used to join a prefix to a root word, if adding it helps the reader with pronunciation. If the prefix ends in a vowel and the root word also begins with a vowel, a hyphen tells the reader to say two separate sounds. However, there are some exceptions that are never hyphenated, for example, **react**.

Get started

Copy the table. Sort the words into two groups: words that are hyphenated and words that are not hyphenated. One has been done for you.

1. co-worker
2. reactivate
3. react
4. co-star
5. deactivate
6. ice-cream
7. non-stop
8. coincidence
9. uncoordinated
10. co-pilot

Hyphenated	Not hyphenated
co-worker	

Try these

Copy and complete the table, sorting these words into two groups. Write the words that need no hyphen in the first column. Add hyphens to the words that need them and write them in the second column. Two have been done for you.

1. hyperactive
2. retry
3. reheat
4. deenergised
5. uninviting
6. preexist
7. remove
8. ultraawake
9. reenter
10. reenact

No hyphen needed	Hyphen needed
hyperactive	de-energised

Now try these

Look at the words in brackets at the ends of the sentences. Decide whether to hyphenate each word and, if using a hyphen, where the hyphen should be placed. One has been done for you.

1. Sue was always <u>ultra-organised</u> because she had a busy schedule. (ultraorganised)

2. The animals at the zoo _____ peacefully. (coexist)

3. Caroline's new neighbours were very _____. (unfriendly)

4. Isaac and Frank _____ a house together. (coown)

5. Chun could not _____ where she had left her glasses. (remember)

6. To be good at dancing you must have good _____. (coordination)

7. If you are late for dinner I will have to _____ it. (reheat)

8. It is a good idea to _____ before an exam. (revise)

9. The adventure was over; it was time to _____ home. (return)

10. To save their friend, the adventurers must _____ the dragon's lair. (reenter)

The /ee/ sound spelt ei after c

The rhyme 'i before **e**, except after **c**' can help you to spell the /**ee**/ sound, for example, pi**e**ce and di**e**sel.

After **c**, the letters that stand for the /**ee**/ sound are the other way around: **e** comes before **i**, for example, c**ei**ling and r**e**c**ei**pt.

There are exceptions to the rule, such as s**ei**ze and w**ei**rd.

Get started

Copy the table. Sort these words into two groups: those with the **ei** spelling and those with the **ie** spelling. One has been done for you.

1. grief
2. ceiling
3. grieving
4. piece
5. achieve
6. deceit
7. yield
8. belief
9. receive
10. believe

i before **e**	e before **i**
grief	

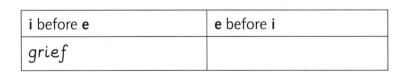

Try these

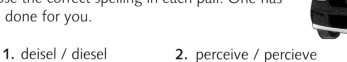

Choose the correct spelling in each pair. One has been done for you.

1. deisel / diesel

   Answer: diesel

2. perceive / percieve

3. hygeine / hygiene

4. field / feild

5. deceive / decieve

6. sheild / shield

7. concieve / conceive

8. brief / breif

9. weild / wield

10. chief / cheif

Now try these

Copy and complete the sentences by choosing the correct spelling of each missing word. One has been done for you.

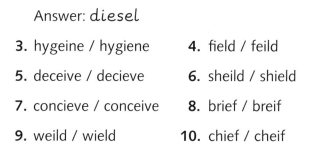

1. The shopkeeper asked if they would like a _____. (reciept / receipt)

   Answer: The shopkeeper asked if they would like a <u>receipt</u>.

2. "Would you like a _____ of cake?" asked Granny. (piece / peice)

3. The pirates dug to _____ the buried treasure. (retrieve / retreive)

4. The mayor is a pompous and _____ man. (concieted / conceited)

5. Zofia _____ praise for her hard work. (recieved / received)

6. The Amazons were _____ female warriors. (fierce / feirce)

7. I am my uncle's favourite _____. (niece / neice)

Common words (3)

There are many words in English with tricky spellings.

Some words have 'silent' letters (letters that don't stand for any sound), such as sol**d**ier, secret**a**ry, parl**i**ament, rest**au**rant and misch**i**evous.

Others have unusual spellings, such as th**or**ough, sto**ma**ch, sh**ou**lder, que**ue**, priv**i**lege, per**su**ade, n**eigh**b**ou**r, n**ui**sance, defin**i**te, l**ei**sure, mu**sc**le.

Get started

Write these words. Underline the letters that are tricky. One has been done for you.

1. soldier

   Answer: sold**i**er

2. thorough

3. shoulder

4. secretary

5. restaurant

6. queue

7. privilege

8. mischievous

Try these

Write the correct spelling in each pair. One has been done for you.

1. parliament   parlament

   Answer: *parliament*

2. perswade   persuade

3. neighbour   naibor

4. nuisance   nusance

5. definit   definite

6. leisure   lesure

7. mussle   muscle

Now try these

Copy and complete the sentences, choosing the correct spellings of the missing words to fill the gaps. One has been done for you.

1. Can I _____ you to come swimming with me?
   (persuade / pursuade)

   Answer: Can I <u>persuade</u> you to come swimming with me?

2. Please give that dog a _____ rub down before he comes inside.
   (thourough / thorough)

3. The _____ was so long that Reuben missed the start of the film.
   (queue / que)

4. Mum will make a _____ decision about the party tomorrow.
   (definite / definit)

5. Uncle Jack has a medal from when he was a _____.
   (soulder / soldier)

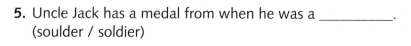

The letter-string ough

The letter-string **ough** is one of the trickiest spellings in English. It can be used to spell a number of different sounds. For example: 'He had a nasty c**ough**.' Here **ough** rhymes with **off**.

Get started

Copy the table and sort these words into three rhyming groups: words that rhyme with **cow**, with **off** and with **huff**. One has been done for you.

1. bough
2. rough
3. cough
4. plough
5. scoff
6. tough
7. bow
8. trough
9. stuff
10. enough

Rhyme with **cow**	Rhyme with **off**	Rhyme with **huff**
bough		

Try these

Write two words with the letter-string **ough** to rhyme with each of these words.
One has been done for you.

1. throw

> Answer: although
>   dough

2. caught

3. scoff

4. now

5. know

Now try these

There are ten misspelt words in this paragraph. Find them and correct
the spellings. They should all be spelt with **ough**. One has been done for you.

Althow *Although* it was sunny, the bitter
cold made Saskia coff. But the wind was
strong and Saskia thort it would be perfect
for kite-flying. The string felt tuff in her
hands as the kite tugged. Suddenly, a gust
ruffly wrenched the kite from her grasp. The
kite dipped and swooped in whirls and troffs
until, suddenly, it plowed into a tall hedge
and became stuck in the bow of a tree. "Oh
no!" thort Saskia. "I'm not tall enuff to get it
down from there!"

Words with 'silent' letters

'Silent' letters are the letters that you cannot detect from the way a word is pronounced. They exist because the pronunciation of many words in the English language has changed over time. Some letters are no longer pronounced, even though they still exist in the spellings.

Get started

Copy the table. Identify the 'silent' letter in each of these words and sort them into the correct column of the table. One has been done for you.

1. knee

2. wrapper

3. knight

4. thumb

5. wrong

6. knuckle

7. knock

8. wrist

9. doubt

10. wreck

'Silent' **w**	'Silent' **k**	'Silent' **b**
	knee	

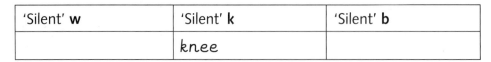

Try these

Choose the correct spelling of each word. One has been done for you.

1. lamm / lamb

   Answer: *lamb*

2. colhum / column

3. gnaw / naw

4. nash / gnash

5. calf / carf

6. ortumn / autumn

7. knome / gnome

8. rhythm / rythmn

9. folk / fohk

10. gnarled / narled

Now try these

Use the words from the 'Try these' activity in sentences of your own. An example has been done for you.

Answer: *The lamb played in the field with its mother.*

Common words (4)

There are many words in English with tricky spellings.

Some words have 'silent' letters (letters that don't stand for any sound), such as cate**g**ory, veg**e**table, ve**h**icle and ya**c**ht.

Others have spellings that are tricky to remember, such as bru**i**se, dis**a**stro**u**s, bar**g**ain, sin**cere**ly, si**g**nature, a**wkw**ard, twel**f**th, var**i**ety, **phy**sical, ligh**tn**ing, f**or**ty.

Get started

Write down the correct spelling in each pair. One has been done for you.

1. vehicle   veicle

   Answer: *vehicle*

2. aukward   awkward

3. yacht   yocht

4. variety   varriety

5. lightenning   lightning

6. signature   signiture

7. sinserly   sincerely

Try these

These words are all spelt incorrectly. Correct the spelling of each word. One has been done for you.

1. fisical

    Answer: *physical*

2. twelth

3. disastrus

4. bargin

5. vegtable

6. fourty

7. brooze

8. categry

Now try these

Use the words below in sentences of your own. An example has been done for you.

yacht, vehicle, awkward, forty, bargain, category, twelfth, bruise

Answer: *The millionaire threw a party aboard his enormous yacht.*

Review unit 2

Can you remember the spellings you've learned this term? Answer these questions to find out.

A. Choose the correct spelling of each word.

1. necessary   nesassary
2. queue   queu
3. enuff   enough
4. yacht   yocht
5. coff   cough
6. bruise   bruze
7. co-operate   cooperate
8. rhythm   rythmn
9. marvelous   marvellous
10. awkward   awquard

B. These words are all spelt incorrectly. Write the correct spelling of each word.

1. thum
2. reenter
3. perswade
4. definate
5. thurough
6. recieve
7. reck
8. fourty
9. ocuppy
10. deice

C. Copy each sentence and write in the missing word.

1. Jill b_____ her PE kit to school.

2. Granny b_____ us an ice-cream.

3. Dad's chin is very r_____ and stubbly.

4. We went to the l_____ centre to go swimming.

5. We hung streamers from the c_____.

Common words (5)

Many words in English are tricky to spell. This unit practises these words: amateur, foreign, frequently, government, available, system, relevant, pronunciation, symbol, hindrance, conscience, conscious, desperate, controversy, convenience.

Get started

Match each word to its meaning. One has been done for you.

amateur, foreign, hindrance, conscience, conscious, controversy

1. <u>amateur</u>: person who does something as a hobby, not to earn money

2. _____: something that is causing arguments

3. _____: aware of what is going on around you

4. _____: inner voice that tells you right from wrong

5. _____: from another country

6. _____: thing that stops something happening

Try these

Cover the words in the introduction this unit. Then choose the correct spellings of the words below. One has been done for you.

1. avaleable   available

   Answer: *available*

2. system   sistem

3. symboll   symbol

4. desperate   desparate

5. relavent   relevant

6. government   goverment

7. contraversy   controversy

8. frequently   frequantly

Now try these

Use the words below in sentences of your own. An example has been done for you.

amateur, conscience, hindrance, pronunciation, convenience

Answer: *Though only an amateur, William was an exceptional artist.*

Homophones and near-homophones (1)

Homophones are words that sound the same but are spelt differently and have different meanings. You always need context (a setting, for example, a sentence) to know which spelling to use. Often, the spellings of homophones just have to be learned. Near-homophones are words that sound similar. They are also spelt differently and have different meanings.

Get started

Match each word to its definition. One has been done for you.

dessert, effect, weary, proceed, precede, affect, desert, wary

1. <u>desert</u>: a lifeless place

2. _____: lacking in energy

3. _____: to come before

4. _____: a sweet course

5. _____: cautious of danger

6. _____: a consequence

7. _____: to influence

8. _____: to continue

Try these

Copy and complete the sentences by choosing the correct spelling of each missing word. One has been done for you.

1. Chloe and Nick are learning how to make a _____. (dessert / desert)

   Answer: *Chloe and Nick are learning how to make a dessert.*

2. Long periods of bad weather can _____ one's mood. (affect / effect)

3. It is very hot in the Sahara _____. (Desert / Dessert)

4. One should always be _____ of crocodiles. (wary / weary)

5. The horror film had disappointingly bad special _____. (affects / effects)

6. The adventurers were _____ from travelling. (wary / weary)

Now try these

Use the following words in sentences of your own.
An example has been done for you.

wary, weary, desert, dessert, affect, effect, proceed, precede

   Answer: *You should always be wary of dragons.*

Homophones and near-homophones (2)

Homophones are words that sound the same but are spelt differently and have different meanings. You always need context (a setting, for example, a sentence) to know how to spell homophones.

Some homophone pairs can be told apart because one of the words is a past tense verb.

Get started

Copy the table below. Sort these words into two groups: words spelt correctly and words spelt incorrectly. Correct the words that are wrong. One has been done for you.

1. herd

2. guest

3. parssed

4. guesst

5. heard

6. past

7. guessed

8. parst

9. heared

10. passed

Correct	Corrected
herd	

Try these

Copy the table below. Sort these words into their word type: nouns or past tense verbs. One has been done for you.

1. herd   **2.** heard

3. guest   **4.** past

5. guessed   **6.** lead

7. passed   **8.** led

Nouns	Past tense verbs
herd	

Now try these

Copy and complete the sentences by choosing the correct spelling of each missing word. One has been done for you.

1. This morning, I _____ my favourite song on the radio. (herd / heard)

Answer: *This morning, I <u>heard</u> my favourite song on the radio.*

2. "May I sit?" asked Sam. "Be my _____!" replied Gale. (guest / guessed)

3. A _____ of cows grazed peacefully in the field. (herd / heard)

4. Captain Smith bravely _____ her troops to victory. (lead / led)

5. In the _____, dinosaurs walked the Earth. (past / passed)

6. _____ is a soft, heavy metal that has many uses. (Lead / Led)

7. No one could have _____ what happened next. (guest / guessed)

8. It was too late; the moment had _____. (past / passed)

Homophones and near-homophones (3)

Homophones are words that sound the same but are spelt differently and have different meanings. You always need context (a setting, for example, a sentence) to know how to spell homophones.

Some homophone pairs can be told apart because one of the words is a verb and the other is a noun. For example, practice is a noun (such as 'a doctor's practice') and practise is a verb (such as 'to practise football').

Get started

Copy the table then sort these words into two groups: nouns and verbs. One has been done for you.

practice   device

advise   license

licence   devise

advice   practise

Nouns	Verbs
practice	

Try these

Match each word to its definition. One has been done for you.

practice, advice, license, advise, prophecy, device, licence, prophesy, devise, practise

1. _practice_: a custom or procedure
2. _____: a permit to do something
3. _____: recommendations or suggestions
4. _____: a prediction of the future
5. _____: to repeat something in order to improve
6. _____: to say what will happen in the future
7. _____: to plan or invent by careful thought
8. _____: to recommend or suggest
9. _____: a piece of equipment
10. _____: to permit someone to do something

Now try these

Copy and complete the sentences using the appropriate term. The first one has been done for you.

1. The doctor's _____ was clear. "I _____ you to stop putting things in your ears," he said. (advice / advise)

   Answer: _The doctor's advice was clear. "I advise you to stop putting things in your ears," he said._

2. "I can _____ the future!" boasted the fortune-teller. "Cheapest _____ for miles!" (prophecy / prophesy)

3. The government plans to _____ the company to produce medicine. The _____ will be issued next week. (licence / license)

4. These days, it is an uncommon _____ among schoolchildren to _____ standing up straight. (practice / practise)

5. "I must _____ a _____ to conquer the world," said the evil villain. (device / devise)

Homophones and near-homophones (4)

Homophones are words that sound the same but are spelt differently and have different meanings. You always need context (a setting, for example, a sentence) to know how to spell homophones. Often, the spellings of homophones just have to be learned.

Get started

Choose the correct spelling in each pair. One has been done for you.

1. serial / cerial

    Answer: *serial*

2. ayle / aisle

3. aloud / alowd

4. draught / druaght

5. prinsipal / principal

6. sereal / cereal

7. isle / asle

8. drafft / draft

9. alloud / allowed

10. principle / prinsiple

Try these

Match each word to its definition. One has been done for you.

stationery, serial, draught, principle, draft, stationary, cereal, principal

1. <u>stationery</u>: writing and office equipment

2. _____: a breakfast food

3. _____: a first version of a piece of writing

4. _____: a story appearing in instalments

5. _____: a current of air in a room

6. _____: not moving

7. _____: the main or most important thing

8. _____: a theory, attitude, opinion or belief

Now try these

Copy and complete the sentences by choosing the correct spelling of each missing word. One has been done for you.

1. Mandeep enjoyed the new three-part drama _____, 'Pirates'. (cereal / serial)

   Answer: <u>Mandeep enjoyed the new three-part drama serial, 'Pirates'.</u>

2. Pencils, erasers and rulers are all items of _____. (stationary / stationery)

3. The cars in the traffic jam had been _____ for hours. (stationary / stationery)

4. Carl is not _____ to go to the match this weekend. (aloud / allowed)

5. We have to write the first _____ of the essay by Monday. (draft / draught)

6. Ava eats a bowl of _____ every day before school. (cereal / serial)

7. An icy _____ blew through the neglected castle. (draft / draught)

Homophones and near-homophones (5)

Homophones are words that sound the same but are spelt differently and have different meanings. You always need context (a setting, for example, a sentence) to know which spelling to use. Often, the spellings of homophones just have to be learned.

ascent (meaning: journey upwards)
For example: Our **ascent** of the mountain was exhausting!

assent (meaning: agreement)
For example: Dad nodded in **assent**.

Get started

Find and write down the correctly spelt word or words in each set. The first set has been done for you.

1. ascent, asent, assent

   Answer: ascent, assent

2. discent, desent, descent

3. mawning, morning, mourning

4. steal, stele, steel

5. who's, whose, who'se

6. disent, dissent, dissant

Which word is a contraction of two words?

Try these

Match each word to its definition. One has been done for you.

steal, descent, bridle, bridal, father, morning, mourning, steel, dissent, farther

1. _dissent_: to disagree

2. _____: headgear for controlling a horse

3. _____: a greater distance

4. _____: grieving arising from loss

5. _____: a male parent

6. _____: to take without permission

7. _____: a journey downwards

8. _____: a hard, strong metal

9. _____: the beginning of the day

10. _____: of or relating to a bride

Now try these

Copy and complete the sentences by choosing the correct spelling of each missing word. One has been done for you.

1. The walkers were glad the _____ from the mountains was over. (dissent / descent)

   Answer: _The walkers were glad the **descent** from the mountains was over._

2. The mayor, _____ face was bright red, spluttered with rage. (whose / who's)

3. The teachers were all in _____ that the trip should proceed. (assent / ascent)

4. "_____ there?" asked the night watchman. "Show yourself!" (Whose / Who's)

Review unit 3

Can you remember the spellings you've learned this term? Answer these questions to find out.

A. These words have all been spelt incorrectly. Write the correct spelling of each word.

1. amater
2. forign
3. goverment
4. conshus
5. desparate
6. contraversy
7. conshence
8. hinderance
9. simble
10. relavent

B. Copy each sentence and complete each bold word, adding the missing letter or letters.

1. Let's **practi__e** our dance.
2. That was a very short piano **practi__e**.
3. The man at the pet shop gave us lots of **advi__e**.
4. I'd **advi__e** you to go out before it rains.
5. We bought a fishing **licen__e**.
6. I did not **licen__e** you to go crazy.
7. The sunshine had a bad **__ffect** on the snowman.

48

8. Kevin's stomach ache __**ffected** his performance.

9. Fergus walked slowly and **w__rily** over the swaying, rope bridge.

10. It was a long, hot drive across the **de__ert**.

C. Copy each definition and write the words that are missing.

1. To go forwards is to 'p_____'.

2. To go before is to 'p_____'.

3. A flow of air inside a building is a 'd_____'.

4. The past tense of 'guess' is 'g_____'.

5. The main or most important thing is the 'p_____'.

6. 'W_____' means 'belonging to whom'.

7. 'F_____' means 'greater distance'.

8. The journey down something is called the 'd_____'.

9. Pens, pencils and rulers are types of 's_____'.

10. A space between rows of chairs is called an 'a_____'.